LIFE

LIFE

DR KRISHNA SAKSENA

Ocean Books
Pvt. Ltd.

Published by
Ocean Books (P) Ltd.
4/19 Asaf Ali Road,
New Delhi-110 002 (INDIA)
e-mail: info@oceanbooks.in

ISBN 978-93-92963-03-2
LIFE
by Dr Krishna Saksena

Edition
2022

Price
₹ 250/- (Two Hundred Fifty Rupees)

Printed at

Japan Art, New Delhi

Preface

Life is perhaps one of the most written topics in the history of philosophical literature, with varying sentiments. Some condemn it "is a tale told by an idiot, full of sound and fury" while others glorify it as the "greatest gift of the Lord".

In this compact book, the author thankfully does not impose her own opinion but rather leaves the reader to draw his or her own conclusions. She presents life from various aspects. That of love, kindness, gratitude, and spirituality with several fascinating anecdotes to demonstrate their impact on the quality of life. I found these fascinating because, just as a picture is worth a thousand word, an actual life event is worth a thousand life-quotes.

I personally found this to be a fascinating read, as the author, with all her simple charm and deep wisdom gently presents for our consideration the various aspects of one's existence. She does not try to address deep existential questions that may delight the armchair philosophers but rather talks about simple truths that can be easily understood and applied in one's own life.

I am pleased to recommend this wonderful outpouring of love

and wisdom from one who has had a long, personal and often tumultuous interaction with life.

– Dr. Dhruv Adawal

LIFE

Money and mansion are
Not the only wealth, hoard
The wealth of spirit.
Character is wealth, good
Conduct is wealth and
Spiritual wisdom is wealth.

Gentleness and goodness are the roots of humanity. One needs to make haste if he has to do good. But one needs to check the mind if evil thoughts come up. For it is to be seen that the mind of one who is slow in doing meritorious action delights in doing evil actions. Rightly so fragrance of flowers spread only in the direction of wind. But your goodness will spread in all directions. Goodness is love in action. All that we are is the result of what we have thought. If you speak or act with an evil thought pain follows. If you speak or act with a pure thought happiness follows, like a shadow that never leaves.

Rendering help to others is the function of all human beings. Try to treat if you meet, an old acquaintance who is now in a bad condition with dignity and honour. "Are you doing good to others? Life's most urgent question is, "What are you doing for others?"

Do not give yourself away. You are so much more than you think about yourself. You are much more than you can see. You are greater than others. You are much more than you have heard about yourself. I want to do so much but nothing makes me happy. When you feel like this you must sit down and think seriously what you want. Then when you are clear in your mind go ahead to do what you feel you must do. What am I doing for others? I must stand in the service of mankind. I come to feel that rendering help to others is the most important job. what am I doing for others? If you help others surely when you need help some will come up for you.

It reminds me of an incident. Once I walked on the pavement of a street, I saw one young man sturdy, healthy and good looking, begging. I went and bought five pairs of slippers. I told him, "You are such a strong, young, healthy man begging. I have brought for you these shoes. You can go and sell them. Whatever you get take some money out for looking after yourself, the remaining money you may use it for buying more shoes which you can sell. So, the profit made every turn will make you live a decent life. I am sure living such a life will make you happy." The young man thought seriously and acted on my advice. Gradually he was successful first in making a small shop then later on a grand shop.

After a passage of time, I, who had given him the slippers came to buy one pair. When I was giving the price, he refused to take it. On being asked the reason, he reminded me, "Sir you are the person who gave a begging young man advice that changed him into a respectable owner of a grand shop." I was happy to hear what the shop keeper told me.

We need to clean ourselves. The real bath is to remove the dirt of the mind. Cleanliness is the control of senses. True wisdom is to see oneness everywhere. God loves those who are pure. Longing for the Lord is like the rosy dawn. After dawn comes the sun. Longing is followed by the vision of God. If you desire to be pure, have firm faith and slowly go on with your devotional practice without wasting your energy in useless discussions and arguments.

If you can smile at life, life will smile at you. Happiness comes from the satisfaction of the soul not from the satisfaction of the body. Those with indomitable spirit are the ones that are a real success in life. If you can so train or condition your mind that you are content regardless of what you have or do not have and if you can stand the challenges of your trials and remain calm that is true happiness. Life has meaning only in the struggle. Triumphs and defeats are in the hands of God. So, we can celebrate the struggle. Violence in principle will be discarded and peace be adopted. This is the only way towards spiritual awakening.

God is at a point where reason breaks down.

We must give sometime to our fellow men, even if it is a small thing, do something for others, for which you get no pay, but the privilege of doing it. Life is something we get after a long time. It is very expensive, so do what the great saints tell us.

But contrary to this idea the great romantic poet Shakespeare tells us that life is but an "empty dream." According to him this world is a stage where one struts and frets his feet and finally the character comes to an end of the stage and falls down, making lot of noise, meaningless. The jewel of the soul is priceless and yet it is being squandered.

Yet another view is given by Osho. According to him the whole life is a play and life should not be taken seriously. The moment you take it seriously you get into trouble. The very root of seriousness brings you into trouble. It is the root cause of anxiety. Take life as “fun! Really life is fun! Certainly, life is nothing but drama.”

“When totally free from outer contacts an individual finds happiness in himself, he is fully trained in God’s discipline and reaches unending bliss.” (Bhagwat Geeta 5.21)

I do not wish to talk about and compare the different views. There is no comparison at all. Yet I will talk about the way stated by Yogis and saints, a life of which we need to talk. Our life we get after a good long time, seeing well that it is not all the time misery. Live with the people who are cheerful so that you can have a little whiff, a taste, a little sweetness that enters your being and you can see a great longing arises in you, seeing that life is not all misery and an empty game. Avoid bad company. At the worst you can live alone. No one saves us but we ourselves. No one can and no one may. We ourselves must walk the path. All that we are is the result of what we have thought. If we speak or act with an evil thought pain follows. If you speak or act with pure thought happiness follows like a shadow that never leaves. Since you alone are responsible for your thoughts only you can change them. You will want to change them when you realize that each thought creates according to its own nature. Therefore, start now to think only those thoughts that will bring you health and happiness.

Money or happiness which is more valuable? If your happiness depends on money, you will never be happy with yourself. Be content with what you have, rejoice in the way the things are. If money helps a man to do good to others it is of some value, but if not, it is a mass of evil. The happiness of your life depends on the quality of your thoughts. It reminds me of a small incident.

A small boy eight years old had a mother who was very sick incapable of doing any work. So, the son would go to a nearby jungle and gather lovely flowers which the mother would stich into garlands which the boy would take and sell them in the nearby Hanuman temple. In the burning heat the ground heated up, so the child was running fast, shouting to buy the flowers and garlands. Sometimes the stones on the ground would hurt him badly. Out of many one fellow felt for the child and getting for him a pair of slippers he offered the child to wear it. Happily, the child took it and put it on his feet and sweetly turned to the one who had given him the slippers and said, "Thank you God." "I am no God." "Sir, last night I told God to give me slippers and here you are to give me what I had asked for. If you are not God, you must be His brother". The man smiled and went away. The happiness of your life depends so much on making some one happy or making someone thankful.

Suffering is a strong teacher. It has broken me, but I hope I have become a stronger and a better person. A man who believes in logic only is like a knife. It makes the hand bleed. The beauty of the soul shines out when a man bears with composure one heavy mischance after another, and he is a man of high and heroic temper.

There is no division of east and west up in the sky, why should there be so many divisions amongst us. A child of Sudra three years old was standing before the temple and was seen repeating the song that was being sung by the brahmin boys "Om namah Shivai", The mandir pujari came out and ordered the servant to cut off the tongue of the Sudra boy as he had no right to spoil a name that is so sacred. The parents pleaded to spare him and assured him that the child would never be seen near the temple. But the pujari refused to hear. The tongue was chopped off and the child died. Mother died of the shock and the father became a ferocious decoy and went about killing the brahmins.

In another case a child of seven was given a tiffin box filled with food to go and give it to the pandit as it was his grandfather's death anniversary. The child saw a beggar sitting and asked him about the temple. He told him on his one side is the temple and on the other side is the mosque. So, the boy ran towards the temple and found a big lock hanging on the door, so he went to the other side and found a maulvi, standing at the gate. The child asked him who he was and was told that he was a maulvi, a preacher. "My mother has given for a preacher, so please take it and eat the food that is inside it. Today is my grandfather's death anniversary". He pleaded despite Mulla refusing it. "Please take it for you are a preacher and if you refuse it my mother will get very angry with me. So the mulla took it. He then gave the hundred rupees note. The mulla refused to take it and told him that it was meant for the beggar. He then ran back and on the way he threw the money for the beggar. He came home and told the mother that the work has been done nicely. My purpose in telling you these episodes is that an innocent child finds no division why so many divisions with us, the grown-ups on this earth. Togetherness and happiness are not to be found.

As we share the planet earth, we must live in harmony and peace with each other and with nature. This is just not a dream but a necessity. Yesterday is but a dream, tomorrow is only a vision, but today well lived is a happy life. They are forever free who renounce all selfish desires and break away from the ego cage of "I" "me" and "mine" to be united with the Lord. Attain to this and pass from death to immortality. Bhagavat Gita.2.71

Be like a tree that gives shade to him who cuts off its boughs. Express your uniqueness in whatever way you do. Express your individuality. Let existence be proud of you. The life will not be felt as a drag. It will become a fragrance. (Osho) The gap between the Brahmins and Sudras was so great that one would be ashamed to hear that they are all human beings.

We are what we think. All that we are arises with our thoughts. With our thoughts we make the world. You are responsible for your thoughts. So with our thoughts we make the world.

There is a story of the time of Mahabharat when Lord Krishna gave the forecast. After the war of Mahabharat finished, Yudhisthira came for the royal crown ceremony with his four brothers. Krishna told Yudhisthira, “It is My desire you go to the east and observe what all you see on the way while going and returning”. Yudhisthira while going saw that there were five earthen pots. One was filled up and four others were empty. From the empty pots there was a voice coming that they were hungry and thirsty and demanding all types of things. The one that was filled up was attending to all the demands of the four. Yudhisthira went ahead and returned a few years through the same way. Again, he saw the same pots but the change had come. The empty pots were now filled and the pot that was previously filled was now empty and was asking for bread. Four pots were silent and were not giving anything. Krishna on hearing this said that in Kalyuga the four pots represent the children, and the one pot represents the parents. When the children were small, the parents were providing for all their needs. But when the children had grown up and the parents are old and need help, the children did not provide any help.

Few examples are here:--

The husband told his wife that his mother was coming to stay with them, it would be wonderful. The wife lost her temper, "Only two rooms, and if she takes one room, living in only one would be miserable. Her temper I hate. She will be a burden on us. Give her a call that she should not come else I will leave you." At that moment there was a knock at the door. She went to open the door. To her delight, it was her own mother that was there. She embraced her mother and told her husband, "Now there will be no trouble for us. Mom will manage everything for us and we will go about and enjoy ourselves. I will not let mom go at least for three months". Next day when his own mother came the son did not even stand up to touch her feet. After sometime he told his mother to come with him to an old home. He promised to come and take her when his wife's mother would go away. The mother felt insulted and pained and walked back home where she lived alone. She wiped her tears as she entered her tiny lonely abode.

In a similar case a school teacher took her class v children to show how thrown away neglected mothers lived in ashram. A student named Priya was in the group. As she entered the ashram, she saw her Dadi, sad and silent sitting in a corner. With tears in her eyes, she ran and embraced her, "How are you here Dadi? Papa told me that you had gone to meet your friend." Dadi wept and so did the child who refused to go home. When the father of the child came the child told him that she would come only on the condition that Dadi also came with her while Dadi after so much insult would in no way come with him. "One should know what is the right way and will go only on the right way. I live my values everywhere. You need to know my sorrow. There is a court of justice, of conscience. I am here, because I have not loved myself, I have loved the world. Hostile attitude only serves to heat up the situation, whereas true sense of respect cools down what otherwise could become explosive. So, my dear son after so much insult by your wife, you should expect I might come to you, you are mistaken. Please go away and do take your child with you who in her innocence shown the truth of life." "Yes Ma, family is a place where minds come in contact with one another, the home will become a beautiful garden full of lovely flowers. If the minds get out of harmony with one another it is like a storm that plays havoc in the garden". His heart broke as tears came in his eyes.

Money and mansions are not the only wealth. An old lady had two sons one very rich the other poor. But the poor was a man of good character, spiritually wise, always ready to help anyone in need, always worried about the health and happiness of his old mother. A friend of the old lady came to her and asked which son she liked better. "I love both my sons but if you ask for a comparison, I like the one who is poor, for he so much cares for me, so much worried about me and my happiness. My happiness has nothing to do with money. I rejoice with other son as the things are, money has nothing to do with happiness. For me character is wealth, good conduct is wealth and a little service to an old mother is wealth. The greatest gift a parent can give a child during all the ups and downs of life is love. In return the gift a son can give to his mother is loving care during her old age."

Money and lot of property do make you rich and high but sure enough they are not the only wealth. What we must hoard and become rich are good conduct and spiritual wisdom. The devotee engages to the best of his ability into the play of life, fulfilling his role on this earth as a student, employee, husband, wife, parent, neighbor, and community servant but at the heart of the devotee is an intense desire for the lord. Money or happiness which is more valuable? If your happiness depends on money, you will never be happy. We feel that the only thing we need to hoard is money and this will make us happy is the real tragedy of life. You must understand that happiness is of great value. Money stands nowhere near it. But we have thrown it off and running after money. The tragedy of human history is decreasing happiness in the midst of increasing comforts. Just see the birds. They sing not bothered who hears and what anyone thinks. But I think otherwise about myself: MY status, how many buildings I am making, my desire to earn more and more and how can I get name and fame. Money, position I am always thinking, is nothing but a great folly. You do not acquire happiness; our nature is happiness. All that is done is to remove unhappiness. Truly wise is he who is unstirred by praise or blame. Mountains have peaks and valleys. Learning to enjoy the peaks and valleys is a part of wise living. It is foolish to say "I enjoy the peaks and not the valley". In life we have to accept with grace failure and success, then only we are an integrated personality. No one is a perfect person. The wheel of fortune turns round and round and who can say to himself that "I shall be uppermost today".

All that we are is the result of what we have thought. If you speak with an evil thought pain follows. If you speak or act with a pure thought happiness follows like a shadow that never leaves.

Since you alone are responsible for your thoughts, only you can change them. You would like to change them when you realise that behind each thought there is a different feeling. Since you alone are responsible for your thought, only you can change them. You want to change them when you realise that each thought creates according to its own nature. Therefore, start now to think only those thoughts that will bring you happiness and health. The happiness of your life depends on the quality of your thoughts. Take care that you entertain no notions that are unsuitable for you and against virtue.

Truly wise is he who is not disturbed by praise or blame, by love or hatred. He delights in the blissful self. When we feel high, we have no problems. The problem comes when we feel low. No one wants to feel low. When we want to feel high the low feelings still persist. This is a big problem. Do not simply follow your feelings till you feel clear in your mind. When you arrive at the stage of clarity you are able to shift your perspective by viewing a situation in a new light.

Keep your face always towards the sunshine and shadows will fall behind you. Have faith in God. It is the spirit that sustains life. Faith is the ray of sunshine that lights up the dark, deep caverns of human life. Render help to another is the function of all human beings.

It was not devastation or death that won the day. It was humanity that triumphed. The shining victory of generosity courage and love. A boy warned the people of a tiger that was let lose at night from his cage. Rendering help to another is the function of all beings. Let love of brothers continue. Do not neglect to show hospitality to strangers. By this some have entertained God without knowing it. Selfless service alone has given the needed strength and courage to awaken the real you sleeping inside your heart. Freely we serve because freely we love.

After a hard day of work, the night gives us an opportunity to take rest and relax. Thus, our batteries are recharged and we are ready for the challenges of the next day. The transition brings a blissful life without worries. We experience a joyful life, a thoughtless state of being, full of peace and contentment. Life is without fear and anxiety. Keep away from those who are a negative influence in your life. Keep the company of spiritual books, elevated thoughts and develop your intellect through evolved people.

All evils are expression of ignorance of spiritual knowledge. Just as a doctors begin with symptomatic treatment of diseases but slowly work to eradicate the very cause of diseases, we must eradicate spiritual ignorance to treat our social ills. It is the vision that makes all the difference. A narrow vision is divisive, a broad vision is expansive but a spiritual vision is all inclusive.

You say “He lost his life” or “my life” as if life was something you can possess or lose. The truth is “You do not have a life. You are life. The One Life, the one consciousness that pervades the entire universe and takes a temporary form to experience itself as a stone, animal, person, or so many other things.”

Rain clouds come floating, not to muddy the days ahead, but to make it calm, happy and hopeful. We cannot just shy away from challenges we meet every day. Life is a battle and rightly so as each day we come up with new set of problems which we have to meet with courage. The self-confidence one builds from achieving difficult things and accomplishing goals is the most beautiful thing.

Compassion is like fragrant gold _

its value is inexpressible. Therefore go among the sad and suffering, love the poor and pained with all your heart. Our greatest obligation in this world is to serve others.

John Rockefeller was the richest man of the world. The first billionaire of the world. By the age of 25 he controlled one of the largest refineries in U.S. By the age of 31 he became the largest refiner. As times went on, he kept on climbing the ladder of success. As a young man every decision, attitude, and relationship were tailored to create his personal power and wealth. BY 53 years of age, he became ill. His body shook with severe pain and he lost all his hair. In complete agony the world's only billionaire who would buy anything he wanted had to be satisfied with only soup and crackers. An associate wrote "He could not sleep, would not smile, and would not do anything and meant nothing in life as meaningful". His highly skilled predicted that he would die within a year. The year passed agonizing slowly. As he approached death, he woke up one morning with a vague realization of not being able to take any of his wealth with him into the next world. The man who could control the business world, was not in control of his own life. He was left with a choice. He called his attorneys, accountant, managers, and announced that he wanted to channel his assets; hospitals, research and charity work. John Rockefeller established his foundation. The new direction eventually led to the discovery of penicillin, cures of malaria, tuberculosis, and diphtheria.

But the most amazing part of Rockefeller's story is that the moment he began to give back a portion of all he earned, his body's chemistry changed, it was altered.

He got better. It looked as he would die. But he lived to be 98.

Rockefeller learned gratitude and gave a vast portion of his property to the needy.

Doing so made him whole.
It is one thing to be healed,
It is another thing to be made whole.

Before his death, he wrote in his diary:

The super energy taught me that everything belongs to Him and I am only a channel to comply

His wishes. "My life has been one long holiday. Full of work and full of play. I dropped the worry on the way. And God was good to me every day".

He learnt from his mistake. Running after money should not be our goal of life. For people money is the most important thing. So naturally madly they are after it. Ma Lakshmi observing this became too proud of herself and told her husband, Lord Vishnu, "See all are running after me and none is bothered about you. If you have any doubt, we can have a ride all round and see things ourselves." Lord Vishnu agreed, and both sat on a chariot and started. As Ma Lakshmi started throwing coins any number was found running after the chariot. Ma with great pride turned to Lord Vishnu and said, "See the truth of my statement". The lord was quiet. After sometime a dead body was found lying on the ground.

Ma Lakshmi threw lot of coins on him, but he did not even stir an inch. Lord Vishnu smiled and said, "He will not get up to gather your gift because I am not within him. Your importance will be where I am there. If we cannot raise and surrender ourselves to the Divine all our wealth and numerous mansions will be of no good. A philosopher when asked to count, would count up to number twelve but when he came to thirteen, he would stop and keep on repeating "tera, tera, tera" he would go into trance and could not come out of it.

Swami Vivekanand is not different from any one of us. If he could rise so high to attain spiritual elevation, why can't we? Despondency is the real stumbling block in us. We are endowed with all the powers of mind and soul like him. Despondency, if removed, our path is easy, smooth and within us we develop a feeling of surrender.

It is we that make our destiny, so our future depends on us. Spirit never gets old. Spirituality and age do not go together. One feels young spiritually at all stages of life. So, all of us can attain anything in spiritual field and it is never too late.

There was a severe famine in a village. In a room there was a family of five. Mongoose was also there sitting in the corner. There was a knock at the door. On opening the door there was a sadhu. He was very hungry. He asked for food. They had cooked few chapattis which was sufficient for only one, which they decided they all will share but all the five members, one by one gave their share of food to the sadhu as he was hungry. A little rice that was left after sadhu had gone was shared by all the five. After eating they washed their hands and shook to throw the water off. It fell on half the side of the mongoose which became golden. Ever since then he has been waiting for some other place where his whole body may become golden.

Yudhishter performed a yagya on a vast scale. He invited many to come for the feast

All arrangements were made that were of high scale. The grand gesture of giving gifts was performed. All round there was high praise for the beautiful performance. Mongoose saw this yagya and commented "This is no yagya, where there is no spirit of sacrifice. Where there is plenty one can easily give. I have nowhere seen a place that can make half remaining body golden."

In another case a woman was making breads for her husband when a very hungry woman passed by and begged for few as she was starving. She asked her to wait. She was happy and sat down. She went inside and got a jar of water boiled and came outside and poured it on the woman. Crying loudly with pain she ran off. "I have taught her a lesson, not to beg." She commented.

There lived in the city of Alwar a family of a poor brahmin Purshotam. He had his wife Kamla Devi and his five-year child Shiv. Though they had very little to live upon they were very happy. Purshotam with his family would take the meals together. At night Purshotam would teach Shyam important things which he must practice in life. "In the morning when you get up the first thing you need to do is to go to the Puja room and with folded hands bowing down say "Jai Mata", after which go and touch the feet of your mom. Then you begin the day. Learn your lessons and if there is any difficulty you can ask me." At night Shyam would lie down with his father and ask questions. Once he asked, "Papa, why is the sun so bright and hot and moon so cool and so dim". "You see my child, the moon, bowing down is begging from the sun so it gets cool. A beggar cannot get heated up. Also, a beggar would get as much light as the giver wants, so the moon is at the mercy of the sun."

Shyam was a brilliant student as he grew up. He passed M.A. in first division. Father had gone sick after retirement. There was no money for good treatment, so he passed away. A very happy family lost its glamour as the mother had to go and wash utensils in three families. Shyam was trying his best to find a job. As luck would have it, a job of an assistant manager came out. He applied for it. Quite a number also applied. All the candidates were in fashionable dresses but poor Shyam was in kurta pyjama which he had washed for the interview. A huge bundle was kept there. An aged man came and stood by the side of bundle, looking on all sides for help. No one came forward. It was shyam who came forward and said “May I help you, sir”. The man replied, “Please put this bundle in the bag on my back”. Shyam took the bag and put bundle and reached it to his room. The gentleman was highly impressed by Shyam. He remembered the teaching of his father that an elderly man needs to be respected and helped. He did very well in the examination and interview. He was selected. Also accommodation was given. The first thing Shyam did was to bring his mother and made her to sit on a chair, and put his head on her feet. "Ma, you have done so much for me, now my turn." Then he ran to say, "Jai Mata". He did hard work and made a good hospital free for the poor and the unprivileged. But he could never forget his father. He died without medicine and without money. He could make his mother happy and comfortable but what about his papa. He had gone and is no more. He had gone but he could be made comfortable if his words were followed. "Do meditation, it is just a courage to be silent and alone. Slowly you will start feeling a new quality to yourself, a new aliveness, a new beauty, a new intelligence, which is not borrowed from anybody, which is growing within you. It has roots in our existence. If you make money keep some for yourself and some should be used for the poor and needy. There should be humility in all your dealings. In doing all this you need always to remember the Mother Divine. Proceed with these qualities in life and I can always be proud of you and bless you from wherever I am."

In another example, a poor man came to one town looking for work.

There was another man in the town also. The poor man requested the man to give him some food for he was very hungry. The man replied that he had some wool with which he was weaving. He could take the wool and sell it in the market and out of the money he could buy something to eat. The poor man readily agreed and took the wool and went off. But while going to the market on the way was a pool where there were many fishes. An idea stuck him. He used the wool to knit a net and then to catch the fishes. He sold the fishes in the market and made good money. With that money he started a business and became a rich person. He once came over to thank the man who gave him the wool. However, the man felt very sad and told him that he was responsible for taking so many lives of the fishes. Thus, in this affair he felt that he was a sinner who was equally to be blamed because he was a partner in the business.

Last but not the least was the surprise of Arjun when he saw disaster all round. Everything destroyed, he was sad that the world had at last come to an end. It is being extinguished and such a beautiful creation will no more be there. When he was in such a pensive mood, to his surprise and joy he saw in the midst of all this disaster a sweet, fresh, pretty green stem blooming telling us that this circle will go on forever and forever.

❑